NOSTRADAMUS

A Life From Beginning to End

Copyright © 2017 by Hourly History.

All rights reserved.

Table of Contents

Introduction
Humble Origins
Early Years as a Doctor
Altercation with the Inquisition
The Start of the Occult
Hiding His Predictions
The Prophet of Satan
Continued Work until Death
Nostradamus' Predictions
Sharlatan or Visionary
Nostradamus' Legacy
Conclusion

Introduction

Michel de Nostredame, better known via the Latin form Nostradamus, is perhaps the most famous seer that has ever existed. He may have died 450 years ago, but even today individuals turn to his works and prophecies to interpret them in accordance with modern day events.

It is claimed that he foresaw events such as the September 11 attacks, the Arab Spring, World War Two, and so many other global events that it's now commonplace for individuals to turn to his writings to determine if he had indeed foreseen these happenings centuries before they occurred.

The question on everyone's mind remains; is it even possible for such a thing to happen? Is it feasible for an individual to prophesy these occurrences thanks to the power of observing the stars and planets? That is something we will have to look into throughout the course of this book on Nostradamus. We will also dive into other questions looming in the horizon; who exactly was he? Who was the man behind the name and how exactly was he able to apparently see into the future? What was his background and why is he so famous today? Was he a one-off, or is something else going on?

His story is one that is far more intricate and complicated than you may imagine. It is one that may not even be as straight-forward or accurate as you believe. It might even be the case that Nostradamus was pulling the wool over our eyes for centuries with it only becoming apparent now.

So, let us delve into the background of this man, and begin to piece together his life story and the way in which he is now viewed in popular culture all around the world.

Chapter One

Humble Origins

"Nothing in the world can one imagine beforehand, not the least thing, everything is made up of so many unique particulars that cannot be foreseen."

—Nostradamus

The tale of this amazing individual begins in 1503 in a small commune called Saint-Remy-de-Provence in the south of France. It was here that Nostradamus was born on December 14—although some sources say it was December 21—into a family that, while not the richest in the area, was certainly relatively well-off compared to most. It may not have been the most auspicious of starts, but he would go on to make the absolute most of his situation.

His father was primarily a grain dealer, but also served as a notary. Even though the family was originally Jewish, they had converted to Catholicism a couple of generations prior. Considering the way in which Nostradamus would ultimately make his mark in the world, it's surprising to discover that we know very little about his earliest years. Indeed, to pull together the snippets of information requires a certain degree of detective work, and even then, the picture is relatively incomplete. Thankfully, the information that we do have is relevant to the overall story.

What we are aware of is that he was one of nine children. His father went by the name of Jaume de Nostredame, although the name itself was relatively new. Previously, his grandfather had been forced into changing the name to hide their Jewish descent to avoid falling foul of the Inquisition. This was a dangerous time, with religious persecution being widespread, for any family that was not following the concept of the Catholic Church. It would be a bold move to change their surname, and who knows how different the world would have been if this action had not been taken.

It is clear that Nostradamus was regarded as being an intelligent child. At first, it is believed he was tutored at home by his maternal grandfather, Jean de St Remy, and it was he that first picked up on the fact that the young Nostradamus was potentially a gifted child.

Studies have shown that Nostradamus was introduced to subjects such as Hebrew, Greek, and Latin as well as mathematics, subjects that would stand him in good stead for later in life. He long viewed his grandfather as being a decisive force in his life, and it is tricky to understand how things may have panned out without his early intervention.

However, considering what would follow in his life, it was the introduction to the ancient art of astrology that captured the imagination of the young Nostradamus. Immediately, this celestial science was able to spark a fire inside his stomach that would burn continuously throughout his life. A fire to try to understand the heavens and the role that they would play in determining the destiny of humans—something which he is still known for centuries after his death.

Due to his bright intellect, it is no surprise to discover that Nostradamus followed the path of further education. By the time he was 14, we find him having enrolled at the University of Avignon in order to study medicine. Rather unfortunately for him, his first attempt at studying medicine was cut short a mere 12 months later as the bubonic plague made yet another appearance in this part of the world. The plague and Nostradamus would cross each other's paths again in the future.

During this break in his studies, Nostradamus himself tells us that he went on a journey through the French countryside to further expand his knowledge. He took this opportunity to learn more about herbal medicine and was fortunate enough to spend a period of time working as an apothecary. This provided him with a greater insight into the world of medicine, and there is no doubt that it shaped a lot of his future decisions. This chapter of his life would change the way in which he tackled various illnesses throughout his time as a physician. In some ways, he was ahead of his generation quite considerably.

As we reach 1522, we find Nostradamus seeking to resume his studies. However, this time it was not at the University of Avignon. Instead, he had shifted his focus to the University of Montpelier, although he still had the intention of studying medicine and claiming his doctorate.

Even though he was clearly gifted in this field, it appears that his time spent as an apothecary mixed in with his strong beliefs on the values of astrology meant that he developed the habit of running into problems with the Catholic priests that ran the university. Some sources state that he was expelled from the school although others claim that this was not the case with him being granted permission to become a medical doctor in 1525. It would not be the first time that he would end up on the wrong side of the religious authorities.

It was at this point that Michel de Nostredame took the decision to latinize his name becoming the now famous Nostradamus. This was not unusual at the time. However, very few individuals would go on to have the successful career and make their mark on history like him.

Chapter Two

Early Years as a Doctor

"We need God to prosper those without him will not."

—Nostradamus

After graduating, Nostradamus effectively threw himself into his medical work. He took to traveling around France with his primary focus being on trying to help those individuals that were suffering from the infamous bubonic plague. A brave decision at a time where millions of people were dying from the Black Death all over Europe.

Alas, at this point there was no known cure for the disease. Doctors would rely on various methods that were believed to help alleviate symptoms, although the procedures were to a great extent hit-and-miss given how limited medicine was at the time. Nostradamus took a slightly different approach, and it seems that he did have a higher success rate when it came to saving plague victims. Whether this was more about luck rather than skill is up for debate.

Often, doctors treating afflicted would resort to what we would now see as peculiar methods, including covering the patient in cloth that had been soaked in garlic, and bloodletting as they believed this would release impurities. This fitted in with the Ancient Greek approach of balancing impurities and various aspects of the body in order to counteract disease or infection. Unfortunately, as we know today, it had limited chances of being a success.

Nostradamus was never satisfied with these approaches. Instead, he sought to do things differently, leading to him to focus more on hygiene and pushing for the corpses of those that had succumbed to the disease to be removed quickly. It is hard to imagine that some bodies were effectively left allowing for the disease to spread even faster.

He was also responsible for producing what was effectively a vitamin C pill, although he was unaware of this at the time. The tablet was based on rosehips, and it stemmed from his time studying herbal remedies. It is said that this vitamin infusion did indeed help some of the individuals that had a mild form of the plague, although others claim that it was more to do with him encouraging clean air, a better diet, and improved hygiene.

This was a time where Nostradamus was really starting to excel. Of course, it's not in the area for which he would become famous beyond his death, yet, at the time he was beginning to be something of a celebrity for his success rate. In fact, it could be argued by some that his accomplishments as a physician would inadvertently open the door for his career as an astrologer later on, due to his acceptance into various social circles.

His newly found celebrity status did help him with his still relatively early career in medicine. It would eventually lead to him being provided with funding from a number of locals. In turn, it also brought him to the attention of one of the leading scholars in France at the time, Jules Cesar Scaliger who was based in the city of Agen in the southwest of the country.

The year at this stage was 1531, and after his move to Agen, it is believed that Nostradamus fell in love and was married. To this day, there is some dispute as to the name of his wife, but some sources believe that it was Henriette d'Encausse.

She was to provide him with two children, but unfortunately, this happy family scenario would be short-lived. While on a trip to Italy on a medical mission in 1534, his wife and children contracted the plague and died. Unable to save them, it threw Nostradamus into a tailspin. Also, due to the fact that he was unable to save the life of his own family, it meant that Scaliger lost a great deal of trust in his abilities. He was shunned by the community to a certain extent. Also, Nostradamus was understandably distraught at what had happened, and it would take him some time to recover from the heartbreak and accompanying grief.

His time in this part of France was over.

Chapter Three

Altercation with the Inquisition

"Perfect knowledge of such things cannot be acquired without divine inspiration, given that all prophetic inspiration derives its initial origin from God Almighty."

—Nostradamus

The death of his wife and children hit Nostradamus hard. He had effectively lost his job working in the medical field in Agen, so he is known to have resumed his travels. It is not known where exactly he went during this time, but it is believed that France and Italy were his primary destinations.

The trail of Nostradamus goes relatively cold for several years. When we next hear of him, in 1538, it is under strange circumstances, and not something that you would have generally associated with him.

At this point, it is noted in historical sources that Nostradamus had been found guilty of making some form of an off-the-cuff remark regarding a religious statue. Of course, at the time this was regarded as being a major sin and crime, so he was summoned to appear before the Inquisition of the Church in Provence.

Showing his intelligence, he wisely decided that this was not the best course of action for him to take, as a horrible fate would surely be awaiting him if he appeared in front of the Inquisition. The Inquisition was not something to encounter or mess around with as they thought nothing of providing stern punishments. Instead, he decided to resume his travels once again and would stay away for a number of years, until he believed that it was safe to return.

With these travels, it is suggested by many that he spent time at the more ancient learning schools, which involved a trip to Greece. This could very well be the stage in his life where his interest in astrology and those attributes that he would become more famous for, were honed.

However, it may be the case that his gift for predicting the future was already starting to make an appearance in his life even though he was, as of yet, not too aware of it. To stress this point, we only have to look at one such incident that is regarded by some as potentially being one of the first times where Nostradamus had predicted the future.

There is some suggestion that, while in Italy, he also spent some time with a sect of Franciscan monks. Within this group, Nostradamus is said to have predicted that one of them would become pope at some point in their life. The monk in question was Felice Peretti who, in 1585, would indeed become Pope Sixtus V. Could this have been the start of the prophecies of Nostradamus coming true?

We know relatively little about Nostradamus during this time aside from the points mentioned above. Only snippets of information come to the surface, and even those, such as the encounter with the monks, may not be entirely accurate and may have been designed to enhance his reputation further.

However, what we do know is that he sought a return to France in 1547. Clearly, he was of the opinion that the heresy issue would have blown over by then and that there was nothing to fear regarding the Inquisition. He was free to resume his medical career, but it was his other talents that would now begin to come to the fore.

Chapter Four

The Start of the Occult

"To an old leader will be born an idiot heir. Weak both in knowledge and war."

—Nostradamus

Nostradamus made the decision to settle in a town by the name of Salon-de-Provence. There, he is known to have met and fallen in love with a relatively wealthy widow. His marriage to Anne Ponsarde Gemelle was certainly a far happier story than his first marriage, and the couple eventually had a total of six children.

At this stage, it appears that he was still skirting on the edges of medicine. He dedicated some time to the writing of two medical science books rather than continuing with the treatment of individuals, but he was still involved in trying to combat the plague and help its victims. One of his books focused primarily on the importance of eating the correct food to relieve the symptoms. The fact that another part of the same book also looked at how to prepare cosmetics is just a strange addition that appears to have no link to the main reason for him putting the book together.

It is clear that the plague was still something he was interested in, and he was evidently regarded as being something of an expert on the subject matter. It appears that the earlier failure to save the lives of his first wife and children was now a thing of the past, with his techniques and methods being attributed to alleviating the symptoms of a number of people in the area.

That was the status quo for several years in Salon. To outsiders, it would have come across that Nostradamus was quite content with how his life was proceeding. He looked as if he was happy with his work, yet something new was stirring inside of him. A new obsession or interest—call it what you want—was beginning to build.

That infatuation was connected to aspects of the occult. It would change the rest of his life and also the way in which he is now viewed, leading to us having the individual that the world remembers today.

At first, his interest was relatively minor. It had only been peaked with him, effectively skirting around the edges of the movement and testing out new things. In fact, we are still unsure as to how involved in the movement he was at this point.

It is reported that his fascination began with him spending hours each evening sitting in a room meditating while surrounded by a bowl of water infused with herbal remedies. Nostradamus himself stated that this would help to bring on various trance-like states, visions, and hallucinations, which he would then seek to study and make sense of. For some individuals, these images were seen as being the basis of what would ultimately become his predictions and ability to see into the future.

As he became more absorbed in the occult, Nostradamus was seen to move further away from medicine. He was going through not only a career change but also a life change. By 1550, he felt strongly enough about his beliefs and his ability in astrology to produce his first almanac, something that was used widely by various sectors of society.

Contained within this almanac were his predictions for the year to come. It was also crammed full of astrological information, and it appears that those individuals that came across it took to his writings and sought to look out for the events that he had described. It is unknown as to how accurate he was, but people must have been content with what they read, or he would have stopped at that moment.

Taken aback by the success of his first almanac, Nostradamus decided this was an exercise that should be repeated. He did so the following year, and it would become the second out of a total of eleven almanacs that he would then produce.

It is also important to point out something that is often noted in error regarding his almanacs. Nostradamus would always start them on January 1. Some sources will incorrectly state that his versions would begin in March, but that is wrong. He was seen as being relatively strict, especially when it came to dealing with the basics of the almanac, so he simply would not have made any kind of an error such as that.

The first almanac was an interesting affair. Nostradamus sought to introduce his visions, although they were not the main reason for the calendar at this point. He would also discuss some local folklore, and his almanac was often regarded as being different to many of the others that focused primarily on offering help to farmers and other individuals that relied on the seasons.

This first attempt would become famous across the whole of France, spreading his name far and wide. It was the kind of push he was looking for, and it gave him the confidence that this may very well be a direction that he would wish to follow. At this point, we are unsure as to exactly how many of his predictions from his first almanac turned out to be true, or at least partly accurate, but clearly, Nostradamus was impressed enough with the feedback that he received.

As we said, he ended up producing 11 of these almanacs, but he would also go on to diverge into other aspects that eventually totaled a considerable amount of work throughout the remaining years of his life.

What we find is that this concept of his visions has become an integral part of his work by 1554. Excited by the feedback he was continuing to receive, Nostradamus made the decision to spend more time working on them culminating in what he referred to as *Centuries*.

The aim of this work, according to Nostradamus himself, was that it would involve 10 volumes with each one containing 100 visions of what would occur in the future. These predictions would cover some 2,000 years, which is why so many individuals still refer to his predictions almost 500 years after his death. We are still well within the time limitations as set out by Nostradamus.

However, Nostradamus was intelligent enough to realize that he was placing himself in potential danger by producing these visions. His fear was that those involved in religion would look upon him in an unfavorable manner and there was a very real risk of persecution.

This was not something that would have been taken lightly. There were certainly enough incidents where individuals that claimed to be able to see into the future were treated inhumanly. Indeed, some were killed as a result, so Nostradamus was entirely correct in treading carefully.

Subsequently, he took to disguising his visions, which is why we now have individuals that are still trying to interpret what he is saying and how it correlates to events in the modern world. This was all done on purpose and was not some kind of poetic approach, but merely an attempt to avoid persecution and potential death.

With this approach in mind, Nostradamus went ahead and published a major volume of his prophecies in 1555. The book, *Les Propheties* was intended to push through his primary visions for the future of humanity, with the real focus being on the long-term rather than any insights related to what he saw over the forthcoming 12 months. This is still a book that individuals refer to when attempting to relate to his visions, so it is held in high regard and is an instrumental part of his development as a visionary.

The book perhaps consituted the real beginning of his new career with him being fully involved in his prophecies.

Chapter Five

Hiding His Predictions

"I don't control my vision, they come and go as they will."

—Nostradamus

Remembering the potential danger he was in, it was no surprise that Nostradamus sought to create his own way of disguising his prophecies. As was mentioned in the previous chapter, this was not an attempt to be romantic or to use more colorful language, but a safety net that he could hide behind.

Nowadays, this is seen as being part of the appeal of Nostradamus, with many arguments being had by both scholars and individuals with an interest in his work over what he actually meant in different lines. How did he do it? How could he possibly disguise prophecies and visions? The answer was in the use of quatrains. A word that has now become synonymous with Nostradamus.

A quatrain refers to a verse that rhymes and has four lines. Nostradamus would then go ahead and mix things up even further by including a range of ancient languages within the verse to increase the confusion surrounding what he was writing.

Often, his writings would include not only the true languages of the old Masters— Latin and Greek— but also

Italian and even a dialect from the Provence area of France which was unique to the region. It could be an intricate blend of language and something that Nostradamus took great delight in doing.

Throughout his life, he would go on to produce a total of over 1200 quatrains, but even this represented just a small fraction of his work. Unfortunately, only 946 of them remain today.

To show how he would seek to hide the real meaning behind his quatrains and predictions, we can look at the very first one that he produced. In it, you are able to learn how he goes about getting his visions in the first place, and you will see how even this is written in slightly guarded language.

"I will be seated at night in my secret study,
Alone, sitting upon a stool of brass;
A flame shall leap forth from the solitude,
Granting that which is not believed to be in vain."

Admittedly, you could begin by looking at this quatrain and instantly become confused. However, it is a clever example of the way in which Nostradamus' mind worked and the extent to which he sought to disguise things while only the most intelligent would be able to fully grasp his meaning. The question remains, what does this particular quatrain mean?

It's actually slightly easier than most are aware, but they do get harder to understand the further into them you go, as this very first quatrain refers to the way in which he is able to get his visions. Nostradamus is telling us the process he has to go through, and sets the scene for all of his predictions and insights that are about to follow.

If we look at it carefully, then what we see is that Nostradamus is describing how he enters his study in order to get away from the world and allow him to focus on his visions. He requires peace and quiet in order to do so, but it also informs us how he adopts a strategy that actually harks back to the time of the Ancient Greeks.

Back in Ancient Greece, those individuals that were at the Oracle of Delphi would always use a stool made of brass, with Nostradamus copying this approach. He then goes on to describe lighting a fire and that the visions are leaping from it. Of course, we have no idea how he would have achieved this or even as to whether or not it happened. However, it does give you an indication of how much information could be contained within those four simple lines.

It was an approach that would serve him well and one that he would repeat time and time again for all of his visions, and perhaps it did save his life.

However, one of the more interesting points to make is that Nostradamus somehow managed to avoid running into conflict with the religious figures throughout France. Considering he was effectively looking into the future, which goes against Christianity, it seems that the religious authorities decided to turn a blind eye.

You must keep in mind that this was the time of the Inquisition. The Roman Catholic Church was actively seeking out those individuals that could have been branded as being heretics and, by all accounts, the things that Nostradamus was doing would have qualified.

It's believed by many that the only reason why he wasn't called to see the Inquisition was because he stopped short of performing magic. He knew where the line was going to be and understood how to stop himself from crossing it. Of course, his ability to hide the real messages that he was putting out would have also played a role.

Chapter Six

The Prophet of Satan

"After there is great trouble among mankind, a greater one is prepared."

—Nostradamus

Even though the Inquisition and Roman Catholic Church appeared to have few issues with him that was not always the case with the rest of the world. Indeed, there were a number of individuals that would not just frown upon what he was doing but were actively against it.

Those people believed that Nostradamus was working in tandem with the devil, and it's easy to understand how they would be able to come to that kind of conclusion. After all, religion was the main focus of their life, and Nostradamus was hardly a good Christian with his prophecies and astrological work.

For others, Nostradamus was nothing more than an individual who was, unfortunately, insane. To them, the idea of being able to look into the future was a sign of madness. Alternatively, he was a charlatan and peddling a particular line in order to profit from it. He was not to be believed under any circumstances, and he had to face numerous calls for him to be persecuted or shunned by society.

However, those individuals were luckily in the minority. For most, Nostradamus was someone who was admired and respected, with him attaining something similar to rock star status especially amongst the upper echelons of society.

The fame would ultimately lead to him starting to move in circles that he would have never been able to dream about as a medical doctor. Not only that, but due to his increasing esteem within the elite in France, he saw his fame spreading throughout Europe especially within those particular circles.

If we look at some of the individuals that sought his advice, then one of the most impressive of the time must be Catherine de Medici, the wife of the King of France, Henri II. It is said that she had initially read one of his almanacs and contained within it was a concern that something terrible would happen to the family. Upon reading it, she immediately summoned Nostradamus to her home in order to find out more. Apparently, she wanted to avoid any potential problems and had full faith in his ability to help her in doing so.

After Nostradamus had created a horoscope for both herself and her children, Catherine took the decision to appoint him as her primary counselor, and she also designated him as the leading physician for the health of the King himself. A lofty position for an individual who had gradually moved away from medicine and more towards the occult and his prophecies.

This change in career was certainly regarded as being a sign that he was better received in prominent circles.

However, his prophecies did take a turn for the worse, for the person that was included in it, within royal circles and especially regarding the King.

Nostradamus was concerned about one of his visions that involved the young King and an eye injury. He reported to the Queen that the King should avoid any jousting competition because of the vision that he had previously received.

The vision carried on to include references to the King dying in agony after an incident on the battlefield. Yet, it seems that the King took the decision to not pay that much attention to the advice that was being given to him. Whether he refuted the ideas, or he was not too much of a believer in what Nostradamus was doing is not known. What we do know is that his aversion would end up being a deadly mistake.

Just three years later, the King did indeed die as a direct result of a jousting accident. The lance of his young opponent managed to enter into his brain by going through the space in his visor. It went through his eye, but the King didn't die immediately. Instead, it apparently took him 10 days to die from an infection. This would be the painful and cruel death that Nostradamus had managed to foresee. Or had he? We will cover the potential for Nostradamus and his work not being as clear-cut as you may think later on.

At the time, people had started to see Nostradamus as a talented individual partly because of the way in which he had been accepted into the elite aspect of society. Still, not every person was quite so happy or content with what

Nostradamus was doing. To them, there were other explanations.

During his life, there were some individuals, not only those that were heavily involved in the Catholic Church, who saw Nostradamus as being nothing more than the Prophet of Satan. This charge would clearly be problematic for him especially as this was the time of the Inquisition which we have touched on earlier. To be accused with this name or allegation could have been catastrophic, and yet it appears as if Nostradamus was able to come through it all relatively unscathed. Whether this was due to his connections in the upper circles of society is something that is open to interpretation.

But, why was he viewed by some in this manner? To answer this, we need to look at not only the fact that he was claiming to be able to see into the future but also the way in which he was apparently achieving this remarkable feat.

If we study his prophecies or quatrains, what we see is that he will often refer to some kind of divine entity, and yet he would never name that entity. To those that were religious, it made sense that he must be referring to the Devil because anybody else would surely be named.

Furthermore, a sector of society simply would not believe that he foresaw the future by looking at the stars and planets before relating their position to future events on earth. Instead, they held the firm belief that he was using satanic methods and divination. When you add in the way that he obscured the name of the divine entity, it becomes slightly clearer why some individuals at this time would only come to one conclusion.

It's important to remember that back in this period, if you were unable to explain anything that appeared to be mystical or mysterious, then the Devil would be the likely answer. Also, with the way in which the Catholic Church was cracking down on any non-believers or those guilty of heresy, then fears of the influence of the Devil would have been even higher.

The important thing is that it never appeared to put Nostradamus off his work. He would continue to produce quatrains and annuals throughout his life even in the face of this kind of criticism.

Chapter Seven

Continued Work until Death

"Tomorrow I shall no longer be here."

—Nostradamus

Even though he was not working primarily in the occult field for his entire adult life, Nostradamus was still able to produce a substantial amount of work within this area.

We have already mentioned the fact that he produced 11 annuals, but the sheer volume of quatrains and other prophecies was vast. However, you need to remember that he was not solely writing predictions all of the time. We also know that he was responsible for translating various ancient texts due to his knowledge of Latin and Greek. The library in Lyon has over 2000 documents that are linked back to him, and each one is a translation of an ancient text. How accurate those translations are is certainly something that is up for debate.

One has to remember the way in which work such as this had to be produced. There was no quick fix at all, and it was a long and drawn out process. We also have no idea if all of his work was preserved, although it's difficult to see that this would be the case. It often happens that ancient texts are destroyed or lost, so who knows what else we are missing out on.

There is also the issue of the interpretation and translation of his works; there are many errors within modern day translations. Scholars debate what certain words actually mean in Nostradamus' texts as his language can be rather ambiguous. When you add in the fact that later versions of his work tend to be based on incorrect translations, it results in a complicated situation whereby you can never be entirely sure as to what is his work and what is a modern take on what he was meaning.

The one thing that we do know is that Nostradamus continued working on his prophecies and visions up until the very end. This approach should be admired considering the various health issues that he had, which is something we will now explore.

By 1566, Nostradamus was starting to suffer from various ailments that would eventually lead to his death. Previously, he had recurring bouts of both arthritis and gout throughout his adult life, and this was something that would only go on to get worse as time progressed.

It is believed by many researchers that these conditions evolved into something far worse than before, including the development of dropsy. This meant that there would be an accumulation of fluid beneath the skin and also in various cavities throughout the body. A condition such as this would be painful and troublesome especially in the mid-sixteenth century when medical care had not yet developed to modern day standards.

Nostradamus was also guilty of not actively seeking the correct treatment for his conditions. This approach was certainly unusual considering his history as a doctor. Ultimately, it is known that the choice led to him developing heart failure as a direct result of his condition of health. This development occurred in the first half of 1566. It is said that towards the end of June he asked his lawyer to help him to draw up his will to make sure that his wife and children would be well looked after once he had died.

On July 1, he was reported to have told his secretary that he would not be found alive the next morning. His final prediction came true. Nostradamus was discovered on the floor the following morning after having died at some point during the night.

The discovery signaled the end of his life, but it did not mark the end of his popularity. In fact, it could be argued that his fame is more widespread than ever before and this continues to be the case all around the world.

Chapter Eight

Nostradamus' Predictions

"The third big war will begin when the big city is burning."

—Nostradamus

If you have the spare time and the willingness to do so, then studying his various quatrains, prophecies and annuals will provide you with the opportunity to better understand the main topics that they appear to cover. Also, it allows you to see how Nostradamus' prophecies could be interpreted in a number of different ways to fit in with occurring events.

What you will discover is that the vast majority of the events he discusses and predicts will refer primarily to natural phenomena and notable deaths. Now, it can easily be argued that these incidents will occur no matter what, so predicting that certain events will occur within these two areas is going to make the task substantially easier.

With this, you can perhaps start to see how any individual would be capable of linking almost anything together. Nostradamus also never explicitly stated dates on the vast majority of cases. Thanks to this, you can then take preceding quatrains or prophecies and apply them however you want, and it's still going to make a certain degree of sense.

That being said, he did refer to other subjects and issues within his works, so don't be fooled into thinking that it was only dealing with natural events. He did tend to refer to slightly more specific problems or moments in time as well as technological advances. However, as with everything, this is still open to personal interpretation rather than anything that he said being set in stone. Of course, you can still read his prophecies on your own and see what your personal interpretation of them will be.

One point that can often be overlooked is that Nostradamus was actually a rather spiritual individual. To some, this appears to be a contradiction considering he was doing something that was regarded as being almost anti-Christian. However, aside from his prophecies, he made it abundantly clear that he was a spiritual and religious individual.

You only have to look at one single quote from him which states, "Everything proceeds from the divine power of almighty God, from whom all goodness emanates." It is unknown as to whether or not this played a role in his ability to escape the Inquisition. Although, he did not pass himself off a magician, and as was mentioned earlier, this would have helped his situation.

The problem for Nostradamus was his reluctance to clarify various aspects of his work. He wouldn't attribute the visions to God directly, so for some, there are debate as to just how spiritual he was. In fact, there's a belief in some circles that he was not as religious as he made out.

Just before we move on and look more at the way in which his prophecies worked, it's worth noting that

Nostradamus does have a limitation on his prophecies. That limitation was based upon the end of the world.

It seems he would have just continued producing prophecies, but Nostradamus did look ahead and see something that would stop him in his tracks. According to his writings, the end of the world is going to come after a series of floods and a comet shower, but there's a problem. The problem is in the debate that goes on regarding when the end of the world is going to happen. To some, it will occur only in the year 8555. To others, that is 5000 years too late as they believed that it would end 2000 years after Nostradamus first started his prophecies.

Why do they believe in that? Simply because he wrote down events for the forthcoming 2000 years, and those individuals argue that it must signify the end of the world, or else he would have continued for as long as he could.

It's also worth adding that the phrases he uses to describe the end of the world are ambiguous. He makes it clear about a firestorm, which has to be the comets, but there is no mention as to what happens after it. Therefore, it is left open to interpretation as to whether or not he has included humanity surviving or if it is indeed the end of the world. Only time will tell if this prediction will prove true.

Chapter Nine

Sharlatan or Visionary

"Mankind will discover objects in space sent to us by the watchers."

—Nostradamus

It's useful for us to look at how Nostradamus' predictions worked, according to the man himself, as it provides us with a better insight into his overall workings.

Nostradamus stated that he used the science of judicial astrology for his prophecies. This approach for calculating future events involved him looking at the position of the stars and planets and the direct relationship that they had with the earth. Trying to predict the future in this way was not new. However, Nostradamus was largely regarded as being the individual who took the concept and tried to run with it.

But all was not well. To other astrologers of the time, he was something similar to a charlatan and not to be trusted. Professional astrologers would refer to him as being completely incompetent and that predicting the future could not be done, at least not accurately.

There are some potential issues, as we have touched on previously. A number of people will argue that the reason why his predictions appear to be accurate is simply because of the way in which they are so vague at various times. To some, this meant that they were easier to interpret in any manner that an individual wanted. Attaching them to important modern-day events is made substantially easier as a result.

The difficulty that we have is based on the potential places of origin for his work. To some, it may not be as clear cut as many others would have perhaps previously imagined. Upon studying his prophecies, we do see that the chances of you fully understanding what Nostradamus is referring to are slim, to say the least. This is due to a number of deciding factors that can have an impact on the interpretation.

If we can begin by briefly looking at the controversy that surrounds Nostradamus' prophecies and quatrains, and for this, we need to examine the language that he uses. Often, he will use slightly obscure words from the type of French language that was most prominent at that time. Also, he will throw in references from both Latin and Greek to further confuse the issue. When you combine all of this, it results in it becoming exceedingly difficult to get to the actual root of the point he is attempting to make.

These words will then lead to discussion as to what Nostradamus was actually referring to at various points. A prime example would be the apparent reference to the emergence of Hitler which is often attributed to Nostradamus. Considering this is seen as being one of the most accurate and well-known predictions, it is interesting to note that all may not be as clear as initially thought.

The word in question here is Hister, which people have linked to Hitler. However, Hister can also refer to a particular region near the Danube. Some individuals have, therefore, concluded that Nostradamus was not referring to a person by that name, but rather a geographical area. There are other aspects of this Hister story that people attribute to Hitler, but when we look closely at the wordage, it is easy to place the geographical region into the words instead of an individual.

That is just one example. There are many more, but it could be argued by some that this is part of the appeal of Nostradamus, and that making an attempt to correctly interpret his work is something that we need to get used to. For example, his reference to the Twin Towers attack could easily refer to a whole host of other events. It all comes down to personal interpretations.

However, there is some further controversy that will often surround his work. The issue here is in the apparent use of "end of the world," concepts that come from the Bible. It is argued by some that Nostradamus has taken these ideas, moved them around slightly and then produced them as his own. In other words, there is the belief held by some individuals that Nostradamus was not exactly as he tried to portray himself to society. To them, he was an elaborate charlatan that sought to take the credit for work that had been conducted by others rather than predicting the future himself.

Could it be that Nostradamus was copying aspects from the Bible and merely changing the words slightly? If he is guilty of doing this with his end-of-the-world predictions, then what else could he be up to?

A rather interesting debate surrounds the possibility that Nostradamus was guilty of paraphrasing ancient sources and turning them into his own works. He certainly had the education and knowledge to be able to do so, but whether or not he did is something that must be examined more carefully.

To some, Nostradamus would take known events from the past that did occur, take the text from around the time, and then adapt it so that it could relate to future events that could happen. Indeed, he would often use phrases such as "frogs falling from the sky," or "battles in the clouds," which were almost direct translations from ancient writers.

Furthermore, when he discusses historical moments, it is clear that he has been leaning quite heavily on the likes of Plutarch and Livy with passages being virtually copied from their sources and included in his own text. But, it gets potentially worse.

When it comes to some of his astrological writings, it seems that points that are attributed to him may not actually be his work after all. Indeed, comparisons have been made between his work and details produced in 1549 by Richard Roussat. In fact, there are areas in his work where it appears as if Nostradamus has copied Roussat word for word. It then goes one step further by also covering various tables that he used in order to predict the future via astrology. It seems that even the table was not sacred, with him copying the base of it, and then getting his own aspects wrong at different points.

This is all rather worrying as it does shed a potentially different light on Nostradamus and how he should perhaps be portrayed. It could very well be the case that he is not actually this whiz at predicting the future as we tend to believe. What this now does is it throws open the possibility that vast swathes of his work, was actually down to literary approaches rather than him actively going into a trance-like state. This realization is in complete contrast to what he portrayed, but it is hard to ignore when there is so much research pointing towards him having copied writings from elsewhere.

If you cast your mind back to earlier in the book, we mentioned him describing his approach in one single passage. To some, this is evidence that he did indeed go into a room, meditate, and then see things into the future, and it's important not to turn around and say that none of this happened. It's impossible for us to reach that assumption.

There are aspects of his work that don't appear to lean towards any other influence apart from his own. The only difficulty is in knowing the balance between unique work and that which has been copied.

Chapter Ten

Nostradamus' Legacy

"From the calm morning, the end will come. When of the dancing horse the number of circles will be nine."

—Nostradamus

Are we correct in being skeptical regarding Nostradamus and his predictions for future events? There are arguments for both sides of the discussion, and it is up to you as to which side you fall on. However, it can be useful to examine what the different sides say as part of understanding Nostradamus as we lead towards his apparent legacy.

For those who are against his popularity, their argument is that his fame is largely a modern-day event. Those individuals who support him are viewed as being guilty of manufacturing his reputation by taking his prophecies and making absolutely certain that they fit into events that have occurred in recent history. Their argument is also that his quatrains and writings are far too vague to link them to anything concrete. It provides too much scope to play around with, and it gets tricky for people to argue against the interpretation. The same individuals also draw an important point from the interpretation of his prophecies and quatrains. Not a single quatrain has been interpreted accurately before the event occurs. It is too easy to take his general statements, such as a war starting, and then applying it to anything around those lines. It is certainly an intriguing argument that they make. To them, he is guilty of something called "retro clairvoyance," although it could equally be argued that it was not Nostradamus himself but his modern-day followers that are guilty of that part.

On the flip side, his followers and believers point to the fact that he was forced to hide his real message because of the persecution that was going on in society at that time. What he was doing was effectively heresy, and the penalty for such an act could very well have been death. By masking what he was actually saying, he was saving his own life, and who could blame him for wanting to do this? Others will also argue that he had nothing to gain. The point to predictions at the time was that they were shown to come true.

As you can see, the argument does come from two completely different perspectives. One looks at it from a more scientific and research-based angle. The other focus more on circumstances and societal pressures at the time. Both have their own positives and negatives, but at the end of the day, we can never be entirely sure as to what Nostradamus was doing, or why he was doing it.

Finally, we should look at the legacy of Nostradamus since he is still an influential figure, centuries after his death. It could be argued that he is still very much a superstar with so much emphasis being placed on trying to interpret his prophecies and tie them with events in the world today. It has been claimed that he foresaw various events including the rise of Hitler, the development of the atomic bomb, the Twin Towers attack in New York City, and even Donald Trump becoming president.

However, it is often down to interpretation and how his words are viewed by different people rather than anything else. To many, he never saw these events coming, and his work has been twisted to fit into it rather than the other way around. Even though this may very well be the case, Nostradamus has certainly been able to leave a legacy of some note. After all, there are not too many historical figures that are well known centuries after their death. When you add in the way in which people are aware of what he did during his life—even if it is marginally so—then you do have a figure that has managed to preserve his place in history.

Nostradamus made his mark in the world of his time, and he has also managed to go ahead and make his mark on the world that we know today. It cannot be argued that Nostradamus plays no role or has no impact in the modern world. In fact, as soon as something bad happens anywhere on the globe there appears to be this manic rush to find where Nostradamus stated in his quatrains that this misfortune would occur.

You will also tend to find that a number of media outlets will look at his predictions for the year ahead just after the New Year. Of course, this is leaving his texts wide open to different interpretations, but to many, that's part of the fun of studying Nostradamus and the information that he tends to reveal.

He is a star in his own right. Books that include his writings still sell in huge numbers. Some individuals follow his predictions to the absolute letter or spend countless hours trying to interpret them as best they can. He is referenced in movies, music, popular culture, the list goes on and on, and all of this in connection with an individual that may, or may not, have been able to see into the future. At this point, his potential method is just not that important.

It is hard to see this enthusiasm changing anytime soon. His predictions are too ingrained in our society and culture that it would take a monumental shift that not even Nostradamus himself could have predicted for him to fade from memory.

Nostradamus has to be one of the most quoted individuals in the history of the world. However, this has led to there being a number of occasions where he has been completely misquoted, or people have been the victim of a hoax. This is something that will certainly persist, in particular on the Internet. Nostradamus' fame went viral since the Internet emerged, and as soon as something bad happens in the world, predictions of Nostradamus will be linked to the events. It has actually led to people making up their own prophecies after catastrophes and then passing them off on the Internet as belonging to Nostradamus.

Misquoting can also come from different sources. There are known issues with the original translation from French to English, so it could all start from there. Also, later interpretations or translations of his work very rarely go back to the original sources. Instead, there is a tendency to look at a later edition and work from it. Hence fundamental errors are replicated, making it harder to know which points directly relate to genuine quatrains or prophecies.

The result is that there are phrases or predictions out there that have been absorbed into modern day culture as being attributed to Nostradamus that actually have nothing at all to do with him. He never wrote them, said them, or created them in any form.

If you want to be certain that what you are reading is genuine, then you should conduct some research into those sources that are regarded as being authentic. It saves time as well as brings peace knowing that you can trust the information. Whether you then believe that interpretation is another story.

Conclusion

There's no doubt that Nostradamus led an eventful and colorful life until the very end. From showing early promise as a potentially gifted individual, he continued to show those gifts throughout his childhood studying medicine at the age of 14. His time as a physician was tough thanks to the plague. However, he soon turned himself into something of an expert in this field leading to various successes, even though he failed to save his own family from death.

Nostradamus is best known for being a visionary and a teller of the future. Even centuries after his death, he is held in high regard by a large number of people around the world. They continue to consult his prophecies to match them in accordance with modern day events in order to add some validation to his writings.

Whether you believe his writings and predictions to be accurate or simply down to individuals seeing in his texts what they want to see, there can be little doubt that this is an individual that enthralls and entices us on a regular basis. His name still resonates in this world, and it's difficult to see that changing at any time in the foreseeable future.

There can be little doubt that the intrigue and mystery which surrounds Nostradamus will carry on. He is a figure that will not fade into the background of history. Instead, his works are so extensive and well-known that he shall perhaps forever be referred to when a significant event occurs in the world.

Even if you are unsure as to whether or not the work is his own, even if you don't believe in his prophecies and think it's all a scam; there is something to enjoy within his work.

Made in the USA
Coppell, TX
03 July 2021